The Perils of Patriotism

Facsimile of the Title page
of Judge Henry's original book

AN ACCURATE

AND

INTERESTING ACCOUNT

OF THE

HARDSHIPS AND SUFFERINGS

OF THAT

BAND OF HEROES,

WHO TRAVERSED THE WILDERNESS

IN THE

CAMPAIGN AGAINST QUEBEC

IN 1775.

BY JOHN JOSEPH HENRY, ESQ.

LATE PRESIDENT OF THE SECOND JUDICIAL DISTRICT OF PENNSYLVANIA.

LANCASTER:

PRINTED BY WILLIAM GREER.

1812.

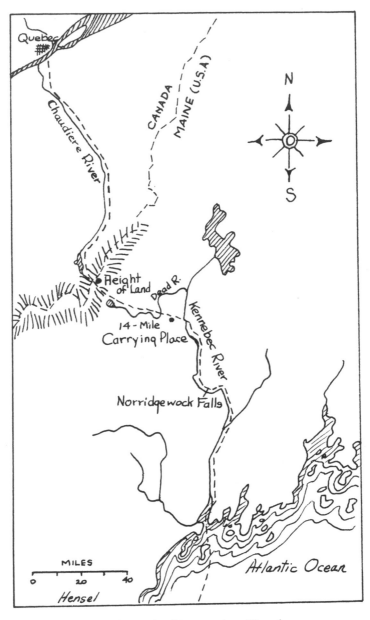

Quebec

Chaudiere River

CANADA

MAINE (U.S.A.)

N

S

Height of Land

Dead R.

Kennebec River

14-Mile Carrying Place

Norridgewock Falls

Atlantic Ocean

MILES

0   20   40

Hensel

Route of Arnold's March to Quebec - 1775

LANCASTER COUNTY DURING THE AMERICAN REVOLUTION

Joseph E. Walker, Editor

The Perils of Patriotism

John Joseph Henry and the
American Attack on Quebec, 1775

by
J. Samuel Walker

Original Illustrations by Joann W. Hensel

Lancaster

A BICENTENNIAL BOOK

1975

The Perils of Patriotism   ISBN 0–915010–08–9

Copyright ℮ 1975 by Lancaster County Historical Society.

Printed in the United States of America.

Library of Congress Catalog Card No. 75–15439

A BICENTENNIAL BOOK *published by*
LANCASTER COUNTY BICENTENNIAL COMMITTEE, INC.
Co-published and distributed by
Sutter House
Box 146, Lititz, Pa. 17543

Foreword

Since the inception of the Lancaster County Bicentennial Committee, its stated major objective has been the involvement of the individual in the preservation of his own rich heritage. We hope to restate the obvious; to discover again things long since set aside or forgotten; to identify that which has been overlooked or has taken on new meaning during these past 200 years.

This book and the series of which it is a part are some of the fruits of that objective. Perhaps it will serve as the inspiration to explore the past and as a guide to make the journey more rewarding.

DONALD G. GOLDSTROM

Introduction

The judge was dying. He knew it to be true, but he had a task which he wished to complete before the inevitable end. He asked his daughter to write what he would tell her. The result was his account of the 1775–1776 campaign of the American army against Quebec as it was seen by a young soldier of seventeen.

John Joseph Henry left Lancaster with the Ross Riflemen during the summer of 1775 to fight the British at Boston. He left his company a few months later to join Matthew Smith's Riflemen, also a Lancaster group, with Benedict Arnold's force to invade Canada. He endured the hardships of the march, the cold of the siege, the humiliation of defeat and the inadequate diet of a military prison. The scurvy he acquired left weaknesses which he never overcame during his subsequent career as a lawyer and judge.

Dr. J. Samuel Walker has recreated in this volume the excitement of a youth caught up in the fervor of war and the disillusionment of defeat and suffering.

Joann W. Hensel adds a vivid visual dimension with her original illustrations of the march, the siege and the prisoners.

This book is the fourth in a series planned to show various aspects of Lancaster County life during the American Revolution. Earlier volumes have discussed social life, the Pennsylvania rifle and military participation in the war. Projected issues will show the service of supply, political leaders and objectors to the war—political and religious.

THE EDITOR

The Perils of Patriotism

$\mathcal{F}$OR JOHN JOSEPH HENRY, age sixteen, the early days of the American Revolution were times of intoxicating excitement. Born in Lancaster, Pennsylvania, in 1758, he grew up during the period of growing conflict and deepening discord between the American colonies and England. Both his father, a respected gunsmith in Lancaster, and his mother were ardent patriots, and young Henry was raised in an atmosphere of defiance toward the mother country. The elder Henry wanted his son to follow his footsteps by becoming a gunsmith, but John Joseph yearned for more venturesome pursuits.

In the summer of 1775, a short time after the battles of Lexington and Concord, young Henry joined the James Ross Company of riflemen, formed in Lancaster County to march to the relief of Boston. He enlisted without the knowledge of his father, but he shared the secret with his mother, who clandestinely fashioned him a uniform—a hunting shirt, leggings, and moccasins. Henry's ruse was nearly exposed on the day the company left home. The troops were lined up for inspection, and among those who reviewed the militia was none other than his own father. To Henry's vast relief, his father failed to recognize him in his rifleman's outfit, and he marched off with his fellow Lancastrians. Soon after arriving in Massachusetts, he defected from the Ross Company to join the forces Colonel Benedict Arnold was gathering for an attack on Quebec, Canada.

Plans for the Quebec Campaign

There must have been times in the following months that Henry wished his father had recognized him on the day he left Lancaster, because the wrath of his father could not have exceeded the privation, hardships and suffering he endured on the ill-fated campaign to take

Quebec. Henry waited 35 years to record his recollections of the expedition to Canada, and the long span of time frequently clouded his memory and colored his judgments. But the account of his journey that he completed in 1811 was nevertheless a vivid and compelling tale of a critical episode in the history of the American Revolution.

The march to Quebec under the command of Benedict Arnold was a part of an overall American plan to conquer Canada. Even as Arnold was gathering and organizing his forces in Cambridge, Massachusetts, an army of 1700 men under General Richard Montgomery was proceeding northward from New York to attack Montreal.

The American colonists mounted the campaign against Canada for a number of important reasons. They had been outraged by the Quebec Act of 1774, in which the British had extended the boundaries of Canada far south to include all land north of the Ohio River between the Allegheny Mountains and the Mississippi. Many Americans coveted that territory and were anxious to nullify the obnoxious Quebec Act. Since Canada did not have a representative government elected by the people, they also feared being encircled in the north and west by a despotic regime still loyal to the king. Therefore, they were hopeful that the Canadians would join the rebellion against England, thus demonstrating colonial solidarity against the mother country. Many Americans envisioned Canada as a fourteenth colony that would help defeat England and unite with the other colonies as a part of a single independent country. Americans also viewed control of Canada as vital to achieving military victory over Britain. They feared—and subsequent events justified their anxieties—that the British would use Canada as a base from which to drive southward in an attempt to isolate New England from the other colonies. If the colonies could be so divided, it would be much easier to crush the rebellion.

During the early part of September, 1775, Benedict Arnold labored to raise and organize an army to march on Quebec. He recruited ten companies of volunteers from the American forces stationed in Cambridge, comprised mostly of men who were bored with the lack of action and excitement in the Boston area. They were joined by three companies of riflemen, one from Virginia and two from Pennsylvania. The Virginia unit was commanded by Captain Daniel Morgan, an exceptional leader who clothed his imposing six-foot, two hundred-pound frame in white buckskins. A veteran of Braddock's march during the French and Indian War, he never forgot the five hundred lashes he once received as punishment for striking a British officer.

Captain William Hendricks led a company from Cumberland County, Pennsylvania, and Captain Matthew Smith headed the 87 member Lancaster contingent of which John Joseph Henry was a part. Smith was an experienced militia officer whose exploits included participation with the Paxton Boys in the bloody massacre of a group of peaceful Indians in Lancaster County. He had also been a leader when the Paxton Boys marched on Philadelphia in 1764 to demand that the colonial government take effective action to protect the frontier from Indians. Henry recalled that Smith "was a good looking man," with "the air of a soldier," but who "was illiterate and outrageously talkative." Altogether the thirteen companies totaled about 1050 men.

Although Benedict Arnold is best remembered as a turncoat who betrayed his country for the promise of a large sum of money, in the early days of the American Revolution he was one of the colonists' most able and promising leaders. Thirty-four years old in 1775, he was charming, courageous and ambitious, and inspired enough confidence in General George Washington to win command of the expedition to Quebec. Henry remembered Arnold as a man of "remarkable character" who "was brave, even to temerity" and "was beloved by the soldiery." But he was quick to add that Arnold was "sordidly avaricious," a judgment that doubtlessly stemmed from Arnold's subsequent treason rather than from the opinions Henry held at the time.

Arnold planned to lead his forces over a difficult route to Quebec. The Americans would travel northward on the Kennebec River, located in the present-day state of Maine. While most of the men tramped through the wilderness along the river, food, supplies and ammunition would be transported on a fleet of small, flat-bottomed boats called bateaux. In places where the river was impassable because of rapids, waterfalls and other obstacles, the boats and their cargo would be carried overland. After going over a hundred miles on the Kennebec, the army would reach a long portage called the "Great Carrying Place." Here the troops would lug the bateaux and equipment over fourteen miles of rugged terrain before arriving at the Dead River, so named because of the alleged calmness of its waters. The Dead River flowed westward and would deposit the troops at the "Height of Land," a steep and formidable extension of the Appalachian Mountains. Once the hills were traversed, the army would journey northward to Quebec on the fast-flowing Chaudière River, which lived up to the English translation of its name—caldron.

A leader less bold and impetuous than Benedict Arnold would have shrunk from the idea of transporting an army over such prohibitive

Arnold's men start up the Kennebec in bateaux.

obstacles. The march to Quebec was, after all, merely a prelude to the even more arduous task of storming and conquering the city itself. Both Arnold and Washington underestimated the pitfalls and hardships of the planned journey; the information on which they based their judgments was imperfect and misleading. They would probably not have suspended their plans even if their knowledge of the Kennebec route had been more complete. But they would surely have been more careful in their preparations if they had realized the severe difficulties the American troops would face in the wilderness. General Washington wrote to the Continental Congress on September 21, 1775, "I have detached Col. Arnold, with one thousand men, to penetrate into Canada by way of Kennebec River and, if possible, to make himself master of Quebec. . . . I have made all possible inquiry as to the distance, the safety of the route, and the danger of the season being too far advanced, but have found nothing in either to deter [the march] from proceeding."

From Boston to the Kennebec

The expedition got under way on September 11, 1775, when the first detachments of soldiers left Cambridge and marched fifty miles to Newburyport, Massachusetts. Once all the troops had reached Newburyport, they sailed northward across a brief stretch of ocean waters and arrived at Gardinerstown, near the mouth of the Kennebec River, on September 22.

In Gardinerstown, a shipbuilder named Reuben Colburn had supervised the construction of the two hundred bateaux that the army would use on its journey to Quebec. Colburn had performed a remarkable feat in building the boats in less than three weeks, but the quality of the workmanship had suffered badly in the rush to complete the project. Without an adequate supply of seasoned lumber on hand, Colburn had been forced to use green pinewood, and many of the boats were smaller than Arnold had wanted. The bateaux soon proved to be hopelessly unseaworthy. Just four days after the army began its voyage up the Kennebec, one angry soldier recorded in his journal, "Could we then have come within reach of the villains who constructed these crazy things, they would fully have experienced the effects of our vengeance." Colburn was suspected of being a conscienceless profiteer, and, therefore, he never received payment for building the boats. But hasty planning and poor preparation by the

Steele's men shoot rapids in birchbark canoes.

expedition's leaders rather than greed and bad faith on the part of Colburn were primarily to blame for the faulty bateaux.

Henry Joined a Scouting Party

Shortly before the main body of the army embarked on its journey up the Kennebec, Colonel Arnold appointed Lieutenant Archibald Steele, who was second in command of the Lancaster County unit, to lead a scouting party. Arnold ordered Steele to take two fast canoes and ten men on a reconnaissance mission to explore the route between the Kennebec and Chaudière Rivers. He also directed Steele to kill or capture the Indian Natanis, who lived in a cabin along the Dead River and who was thought to be a spy for the British. Among those whom Steele selected to accompany him was his fellow Lancastrian, John Joseph Henry. Henry was pleased and rather surprised to be chosen for the mission. He held Steele, "his messmate and friend," in highest regard, describing him as "a man of an active, courageous, spritely, and hardy disposition."

The scouting party advanced rapidly up the Kennebec as their canoes glided easily through the river waters. The men carefully marked the paths through the short carrying places along the route for the main body of the army following them. After leaving the last settled areas, they refrained from firing their guns and seldom built fires, "though the weather was chilling," because they thought "that this country had numerous Indians in it." After three days, the patrol reached the threshold of the fourteen-mile Great Carrying Place. Here they divided the remaining food among the members of the party, with each man watching closely to make certain the shares were evenly apportioned. "It could not be fairly said," Henry wrote, "that any fraud or circumvention took place." The next two days they made their way across the Great Carrying Place and arrived at the Dead River on the evening of September 29.

Up to that point, the party had encountered no major difficulties, and the mission had been relatively easy and uneventful. But the hardships multiplied and the journey became more perilous as the men proceeded on the Dead River. Since they had neither maps nor a clear idea of how far they had to go to carry out their objectives, they began to ration their food supply carefully by restricting themselves to two meager meals a day. "As we could not obtain food in this miserable portion of the globe, even for money, if we had it, and having nothing else than our arms and our courage to depend on, . . .

Blazing the trail at the 14—mile
carrying place.

yet resolved to accomplish our orders at the hazard of our lives—we prudently began to hoard our provision," Henry recalled. "Half a biscuit and half an inch square of raw pork, became [an] evening's meal." The party did augment their provisions by catching fish, but insufficient nourishment remained an acute problem. They also discovered that the Dead River was misnamed, and its rapids and falls imposed additional burdens and exertions on the weary band of travelers.

After five days of navigating the Dead River, the patrol neared the site of the cabin of the Indian Natanis, the alleged British spy. They landed the canoes a few miles from where they believed Natanis lived and approached the cabin by foot. When they arrived at their destination, they surrounded the house and charged it with rifles cocked. But Natanis was nowhere in sight; he was, said Henry, "wiser and more adroit than his assailants." The men inspected the cabin, and Henry found to his surprise that "the house, for an Indian cabin, was clean and tight." Having failed to accomplish their goal of killing or capturing the wily Indian, the party returned to the canoes and resumed their journey.

The First View of Canada

Food remained scarce, and the weather became "piercingly cold" as the determined band of scouts approached their final obstacle, the mountainous terrain called the Height of Land. Upon reaching the hills, the men scrambled up an Indian path to the top of the mountain. From that vantage point, they could view the Chaudière River. One member of the party, Robert Cunningham, climbed a tall pine tree and described the course of the river for many miles ahead. Thus, the primary task of the mission was achieved, and the men could retrace their route and rejoin the main body of the army, which by that time was moving laboriously up the Kennebec. But the worst trials and suffering for the scouting party were yet to come.

After descending the mountainside in a torrential rainstorm, the men slept under a hastily constructed lean-to that failed to protect them either from the wet or the cold. They arose early the next day and made their way eastward on the Dead River as the downpour of rain continued. For his morning meal, Henry searched his pockets and found a single biscuit and an inch of pork. He ate half the biscuit and saved the rest for later. His companions, whose remaining food supplies were also nearly exhausted, had an equally sparse breakfast. As

Cunningham spies the Lake Chaudière.

they glided along the river, they suddenly spotted a small duck within shooting range. Their unsated hunger instantly overcame their reluctance to use their rifles, and several of the men fired at the unfortunate duck. "A shout of joy arose" as one shot found its mark. That evening the party boiled the duck, but, despite not having eaten since morning, ate only the broth for dinner. "Being young, my appetite was ravenous," Henry remarked, "but honor bound the stomach tightly." The following morning the duck was divided into ten equal shares and devoured. With their strength and spirits somewhat invigorated, the men resumed their journey in hopes of reuniting soon with the rest of the army.

Two days passed with no sign of the approaching American forces. Having eaten the last of the pork and biscuits, the party moved at a rapid pace, but "after a long day's journey still we were supperless." On the morning of October 11, the men's hearts thrilled at the sight of large smoke clouds rising above the trees of the forest. Surely this could be nothing other "than the encampment of the army, our friends, and fellow soldiers." Henry and his mates paddled their canoe furiously and, in their haste, brushed against a large tree branch that jutted into the water. The branch ripped a gaping hole in the canoe, and only with great difficulty did the men keep afloat. They carefully made their way to shore, where they expected to find safety and sustinence among their comrades in the main body of the army. Instead, they found "no army, no friends, no food, only a friendly fire kindled by ourselves as we ascended the river; it had been our camp." A fire that the party had built on its way up the river had continued to smolder and spread, sending up the billowing clouds of smoke.

Now, Henry wrote, the "situation was truly horrible." The men still lacked food, and one of the two canoes, their only means to salvation, lay torn and broken. They had no idea where the army might be, and began to harbor suspicions that it had abandoned the expedition and returned to Cambridge. "That sensation of mind called *the horrors,* seemed to prevail," said Henry. The party utilized birch bark, cedar roots, an empty pork bag and a liberal portion of ingenuity to repair the canoe and, within two hours, set out once again.

They had gone only a few hundred yards when the battered canoe hit a snag, tearing another hole in its bottom. It took another hour to fix that puncture; and, as the men prepared to reembark, further misfortune struck. As one member of the party lifted the remaining good canoe to launch it into the river, his foot slipped in the mud. The canoe crashed to the ground and broke in half. "Now absolute despair for the first time seized me," Henry remembered. "A thought came across my mind, that the Almighty had destined us to die of hunger, in this inhospitable wilderness. The recollection of my parents, my brothers and sister, and the clandestine and cruel manner of my deserting them, drew from me some hidden, yet burning tears, and much mental contrition."

The men patched the disabled canoe as best they could and once again resumed their journey. Acutely aware of the uncertain condition of both canoes, they proceeded cautiously; but their hunger prodded them to move as rapidly as possible under the circumstances. At about dusk, the crew in the second canoe, including Henry, was startled by the sound of rifle shots coming from the lead vessel. Thinking that their companions were under attack, they paddled vigorously to lend assistance. To their surprise and gratification, they discovered that their comrades had shot and killed a moose-deer. "A cry of exultation seemed to burst the narrow valley of the river." The party scrambled to shore, lighted a fire, and within a short time were enjoying a feast of venison. They ate slowly, small morsels at a time, realizing that after days of fasting, rapid consumption of food would make them gravely ill. That night they slept soundly.

The following day the patrol augmented their provisions by slaying an "enormous" bull moose, and a young moose that furnished them with veal. The immediate threat of starvation faded, but the danger had not passed. Although the men had all the meat they wanted, they still lacked bread, salt and other substantive foods they needed to regain their strength. They ate large quantities of meat, but their hunger was unsatisfied, and they remained weak and listless. There still were no signs of the rest of the army, which intensified the party's fear that the main body of forces had deserted them and returned home. Convinced that they possessed insufficient energy to transport their canoes and supplies across the Great Carrying Place, they decided to send a group of three men, led by Lieutenant Steele, to cross the portage by foot and try to find the army. If the party of three located the main forces, they would return with necessary supplies, but in any case they promised to rejoin their companions within three days.

The men who remained behind waited with impatience and growing anxiety for the return of their mates. Five days passed, and still they waited. "Melancholy of the desperate kind oppressed me," Henry recalled. "Convinced that the army had retreated, a prognostication resulted in my mind, that we should all die of mere debility in these wilds." The men resolved to leave their camp, and, carrying their "mawkish food" in knapsacks, began to make their way by foot back toward the Kennebec River. They went only a short distance before, to their joy and relief, they encountered an advance guard of the army. They were given a shot of whiskey, which restored their flagging spirits, and a meal of pork and dumplings, which "seemed a renewal of life." They also learned that Steele and his two companions had arranged for ample provisions to be sent to their camp, "but the bearers, either from cowardice or other cause, never came near us."

Rejoining Arnold's Army

The scouting party had been gone for twenty-six days; and, while they had endured the trials of the wilderness, the army had struggled up the Kennebec. The bateaux had proved to be awkward and unwieldy, and, worst of all, leaky. The poor construction of the boats, combined with a pronounced lack of skill on the part of those maneuvering them, had resulted in considerable seepage and splashing of water in the bottom of boats where the precious supplies were carried. The water had spoiled beef, ruined peas and biscuits, and caused bread to go moldy. But John Joseph Henry and his companions from the scouting mission were delighted to be back with the army. Enjoying good food and warm tents, they soon regained their strength and their "gayety of temper and hilarity." Had they known the hardships that lay before them, they would undoubtedly have been more somber.

The day after the army decamped and began to ascend the Dead River, rain began to fall in torrents. The Dead River suddenly came alive, raging, swirling and overflowing into the adjacent lowlands. While the strongest and most skillful boatmen guided the bateaux down the swollen river, the remainder of the troops trudged through the forest, circling far out of their way to avoid the flooded areas. "This was one of the most fatiguing marches we had as yet performed, though the distance was not great in a direct line," Henry wrote. After marching all day without food, Henry and his companions were dismayed to reach their rendezvous with the bateaux crews only to discover that the boatmen and their precious cargo of food and tents were encamped on the opposite side of the river. "We sat down on the bank sorely pinched by hunger, looking wistfully at our friends beyond the torrent, who were in possession of all the provisions, tents, and camp equipage, convinced however, that the most adventurous boatmen would not dare the passage."

To Henry's astonishment, Lieutenant Michael Simpson of the

Lancaster unit commandeered an empty boat and with amazing dexterity guided it safely across the churning waters. He called for Henry and two other Pennsylvanians to enter the bateau, and they scrambled aboard. The crew shoved off but failed to negotiate the river and had to return to shore. At that point, four or five other men leaped into the boat, ignoring Simpson's warning that the boat could not carry the additional weight. "O God," he said, "men we shall all die." Against all odds, Simpson managed to steer the boat across the river, but, as it struck shore, six of the men prematurely jumped out. The force of their leap pushed the boat back into the swirling river. Swept into the current, the bateau capsized, throwing Simpson and Henry into the water. Swimming was impossible, and Henry thought death was imminent. "Resigned into the bosom of my Savior, my eyes became closed; ... sensibility in a great sense forsook me." Fortunately, an Irishman named Edward Cavanaugh appeared in a boat at the critical moment and pulled both Henry and Simpson safely out of the water.

Henry's life was saved, but his "leather breeches attached closely and coldly to the skin." He was too embarrassed and modest to disclose the source of his discomfort; but, when others noticed his distress, they insisted that he remove his drenched clothing and hang it on a pole to dry. For the rest of the evening, Henry endured good-natured jests from his mates, but the bantering "was borne stoically." Of much greater concern was that he had lost his hat, knapsack and, above all, his rifle. An officer named Nichols gave Henry an extra hat he had, and one member of the Lancaster company who was too ill to continue the march sold him his rifle. Henry had no money to pay for the coveted weapon; so he wrote a note for twelve dollars and charged it to his father. It was "in due time, paid honorably."

For several days, the American forces arduously worked their way up the Dead River. The bateaux continued to leak, and some overturned in the raging waters, resulting in further loss and spoilage of food supplies. Intermittent rain and snow and bitter cold contributed to the miseries and hardships of the journey. Many soldiers, plagued by dysentery and other illnesses, were too weak to continue and had to return home. But the greatest reversal came when Colonel Roger Enos and his Connecticut division decided to quit the expedition. Claiming that they lacked sufficient food to go on and convinced that the rest of the army was foolish for doing so, Enos and his men elected to turn back rather than face the hardships of the Height of Land and the Chaudière River.

Henry awakens to find that a snowstorm
came in the night.

Crossing the Height of Land

The loss of manpower caused by Enos's defection was a serious blow to the army's chances of capturing Quebec. More important in the short run, however, was that Enos's companies took large quantities of the army's remaining provisions with them. They had been responsible for transporting much of the army's extra food supply, and, once they determined to go back to Cambridge, they refused to part with stores they would need on the return trip. Before withdrawing, they relinquished a piddling two and a half barrels of flour to help sustain the rest of the army on its march to Quebec. News of Enos's retreat was a stunning and depressing jolt to the weary and hungry troops who were pushing onward. "It dampened our spirits much," Henry recalled.

The remaining forces ascended with difficulty the mountainous terrain called the Height of Land. They abandoned most of the bateaux at the foot of the hills, but Daniel Morgan insisted that his Virginians carry their boats across the mountain. "It would have made your heart ache, to view the intolerable labors his fine fellows underwent," Henry wrote. "Some of them, it was said, had the flesh worn from their shoulders, even to the bone." By the time the army had traversed the Height of Land, the food supply was critically short. Meat was entirely lacking, and the remaining flour was divided evenly among all the troops. Each man received five small ash cakes that reminded one soldier of "shoemakers' paste." The cakes and the hope of finding adequate provisions in the settled areas of Canada were the only sustinence that the army had as it began its trek down the Chaudière River.

The weak and hungry army struggled along the banks of the Chaudière, alternately facing thistles, ravines, rocky terrain, bogs and marshes. The journey was painful and exhausting for everyone, but nobody suffered more than the drummer from the Lancaster contingent, John Shaeffer. Shaeffer was partly blind and constantly tripped, stumbled and fell headlong over logs, chasms and other obstacles along the route. He was the "laughing stock" of the army, but Henry took pity on him. He helped Shaeffer find his way through the forest and, because somebody had stolen the drummer's ash cakes, shared his meager provisions with him. "This man, blind, starving and almost naked, bore his drum (which was unharmed by all its jostlings) safely to Quebec, when many other hale men died in the wilderness," Henry commented.

In a rather unusual departure from normal military procedure, the wives of two members of the Pennsylvania companies had accompanied their husbands on the expedition to Quebec. Henry described the wife of Sergeant Grier of Hendricks's Cumberland county outfit as "a large, virtuous and respectable woman." Mrs. Grier bore the hardships of the march with admirable fortitude. On one occasion, as the army waded through the frigid, waist-deep waters of a half-frozen pond along the Chaudière, Henry was "humbled, yet astonished" to see Mrs. Grier hike up her skirts and slog to firm ground before him.

The other woman, Mrs. Jemima Warner, whose husband was a part of the Lancaster contingent, suffered tragedy in the wilderness. James Warner was young, strong and handsome but, in Henry's opinion, "a dolt." He had a ravenous appetite and, instead of carefully hoarding his rations, consumed his ash cakes almost immediately. Within a short time, he was sick and starving, and he decided that he could go no further. He sat down at the foot of a tree and told his wife that he was "determined to die." Mrs. Warner begged her husband to continue, and for a time her pleading prodded him on. Before long, however, Warner again sat down, unable to proceed. His wife's tearful supplications failed to move him, and he died during the night. Mrs. Warner covered his body with leaves, took his rifle and ammunition, and rejoined the army. She made her way safely to Quebec but was probably killed during the siege of the city.

Down the Chaudière

The forces who struggled down the Chaudière River were only in slightly better condition than the unfortunate James Warner. Their food supply was exhausted, and some men went days without eating. Upon reaching a sandy beach along the river, several soldiers tore roots out of the ground and ate them raw. Others feasted on a large dog that belonged to one of the men. A group of Henry's companions from Lancaster were so hungry and desperate that they boiled their leather moccasins in the vain hope of extracting a modicum of sustinence. "To me the world had lost its charms," Henry wrote. "Gladly would death have been received as an auspicious herald from the divinity. My privations in every way were such as to produce a willingness to die." Henry even entertained thoughts of suicide, but the "God of all goodness" and the "jovial hilarity" of his friend Michael Simpson drove such notions from his mind.

The army's salvation came on November 3, the ninth day of the grueling journey down the Chaudière River. The advance guard of the army spotted houses that lay a few miles ahead in the French-Canadian settlement of Sartigan. Then the men thrilled to the sight of cattle that a group of Frenchmen were driving along the shore to deliver to the troops. The weary Americans managed "a feeble huzza of joy," and the animals were immediately butchered and devoured. The soldiers at the rear of the army, including Henry's unit, reached the site of the feast too late. To Henry's disgust and dismay, they arrived just as one man "was gorging the last piece of colon, half rinsed, half broiled."

The following day was Henry's seventeenth birthday; and, although the weather was "raw and cold," he and his comrades were cheered by the prospect of finding food. They quickly marched into Sartigan, where they found abundant quantities of food and drink—beef, fowl, hot bread, potatoes, vegetables, rum and brandy. Benedict Arnold had preceded his army down the Chaudière and had made certain his men would be amply provisioned once they reached Sartigan. Wisely, Henry ate slowly and sparingly, aware that overeating after a fasting period could have grievous consequences. Others were less cautious, however, and gorged themselves rapaciously. A number of the men became deathly ill from overeating; Henry recalled that three men from the Lancaster company died from consuming more food than their systems could tolerate.

In Sartigan, Henry and his mates met Natanis, the Indian they had been ordered to capture or kill on their scouting mission. Natanis approached each member of the scouting party "and shook hands in the way of an old acquaintance." He told them that he had followed them clandestinely throughout the scouting mission. When asked why he did not approach the party and "speak to his friends," Natanis truthfully answered, "You would have killed me." The Indian was not a spy for the British; he accompanied the American army to Quebec and was wounded in the assault on the city.

Their appetites sated, the troops resumed their march down the Chaudière. Now they moved easily through settled areas, where Henry was surprised to see "civilized men, in a comfortable state, enjoying all the benefits arising from the institutions of civil society." The native population was friendly to the American forces. The French-Canadians had no love for the British, and many of them sympathized with the rebels' cause. They also welcomed the opportunity to sell their goods and supplies at inflated prices to the American army. Within a short time, the soldiers arrived at the temporary headquarters of Colonel Arnold, located thirty miles south of Quebec. There they found further stockpiles of food awaiting them.

Up to that time, Henry had continued to be fastidious in the amounts of food he consumed. But now, thinking the danger of overeating had passed, he indulged himself on steak, bread and potatoes. Within a short time, he realized that he had woefully miscalculated. As the army resumed its march northward, Henry was beset with a high fever and became "the most miserable of human beings." He struggled to keep up with the other men, though "my eyes, at times, could scarcely discern the way, nor my legs do their office." He slept fitfully that night, and the following morning felt too wretched to continue. As he sat on a log watching the other troops file by, Benedict Arnold approached him on horseback. Arnold called Henry by name and inquired about his health. Upon hearing of the young man's affliction, Arnold hailed the inhabitant of a nearby house and made arrangements with him to care for Henry. Just before the colonel departed, he pressed two silver dollars into Henry's hand—an act that was decidedly out of step with Henry's description of him as "sordidly avaricious."

The Frenchman carried the ailing Henry to his home, where he and his wife attended to him. After spending two days in bed without food, Henry's fever subsided and he regained his strength. On the morning of the third day, the family fed Henry a "humble, but generous" breakfast, and he prepared to leave. The Frenchman "with something like disdain in his countenance," refused to accept the two dollars that Henry offered him. Moved to tears by the kindness and generosity of his hosts, Henry was further astounded when the Frenchman secured him a free passage on a ferry going down the Chaudière River. After sailing several miles down the river and then walking for some distance on "a most gloomy and solitary march," Henry rejoined the rest of the army.

The Army on the St. Lawrence

By that time, Arnold's forces had finally completed their arduous journey and were encamped on the south banks of the St. Lawrence River. The fact that the army even had reached the St. Lawrence was an extraordinary feat that had required enormous courage, stamina and resolution. Some writers have compared the rigors of the expedition with Hannibal's famous march across the Alps two centuries before the birth of Christ. But the men of Arnold's army had neither time for nor interest in self-congratulation. They had surmounted the hardships of the wilderness, but they still faced the formidable task of conquering Quebec. From their camp they could see the forbidding walls of the city rising high above the cliffs that bordered the north bank of the St. Lawrence. A fleet of four armed ships patrolled the river to prevent the Americans from crossing, and the British had impounded all the vessels they could find in the area to keep Arnold's forces from obtaining them. Death, disease and Enos's defection had reduced the size of the American army to 650 men, only 500 of whom were healthy enough to fight. Furthermore, the Americans lacked cannon or artillery with which to assault Quebec once they traversed the St. Lawrence.

Still, the Americans were not discouraged. Their numbers were small, but their confidence and courage were bolstered by their triumph over severe adversity in the wilderness. It seemed inconceivable that the attack on Quebec could present greater dangers or difficulties than those they had encountered and overcome on the march from Massachusetts. Arnold had received information that Quebec's defenses were weak and vulnerable, and he hoped that the garrison would put up minimal resistance. Furthermore, the news from Montreal was reassuring. The American forces under General Montgomery were on the verge of capturing that city; and, once that was accomplished, they would provide reinforcements and artillery for Arnold's assault on Quebec.

Colonel Arnold and his men busily made preparations to cross the St. Lawrence and storm Quebec. They managed to secure about thirty canoes to carry them across the river, and they built ladders and spears for the attack on the city. Meanwhile, Arnold completed plans to traverse the St. Lawrence by night. To his chagrin, heavy winds and rough waters made the river impassable for three nights, and the crossing had to be postponed. Finally, on the evening of November 13, 1775, the wind subsided and the river calmed. Silently, the troops entered the canoes and paddled to the north bank of the St. Lawrence. Since the shortage of canoes made it impossible to ferry all the men at once, three separate trips were required to transport the army across the river. Most of the soldiers arrived safely, but the canoe carrying Lieutenant Archibald Steele of the Lancaster company overturned midway across the river. Other crews fished their comrades out of the icy waters, but there was no room for Steele in the crowded canoes. He grasped the stern of one craft and held on te-

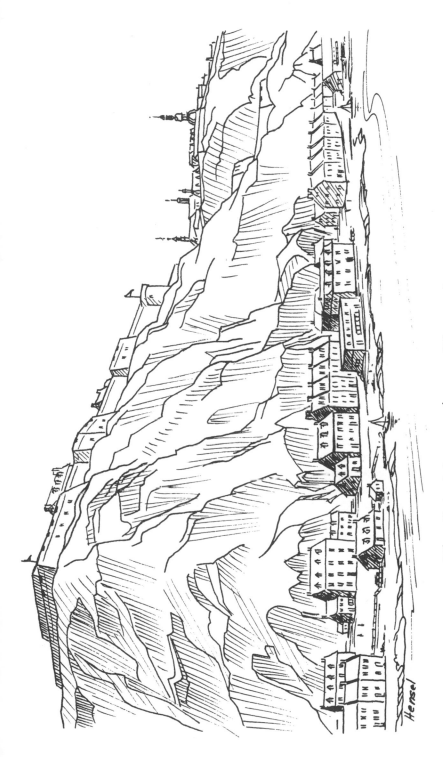

The Citadel and Lower Town of Quebec.

Hensel

naciously as it made its way to shore. Numb, shivering, and "seemingly chilled to the heart," he gratefully received dry clothes, a brisk rubdown and a shot of strong liquor.

After reaching the shore on the north bank of the river, the Americans huddled in a secluded cove. Unfortunately, their crossing did not go undetected. After two waves of canoes had arrived, a British patrol boat appeared and hovered close to the entrance of the cove. Thinking that they had been discovered and fearful for the third wave of canoes then traversing the river, Arnold ordered his men to fire at the vessel. The troops shot with deadly accuracy, and the British ship hastily departed amid shouts of confusion and shrieks of pain from its wounded crew members. The boat alerted the city that the enemy had crossed the river, and the Americans lost the element of surprise they had hoped would increase their chances for victory.

First Encounter With The Enemy

Stealthily, the American forces vacated the cove and filed up a steep incline. By daybreak, the entire army had ascended the slope and stood on the Plains of Abraham, a flat area lying adjacent to the west wall of Quebec. Arnold had abandoned any thoughts of immediately assaulting the city, but he still entertained hopes that the garrison was so weak, unprepared and short on provisions that it would surrender without a fight. He stationed his shivering and bedraggled, but bold and courageous, army on a line facing the wall of Quebec. If Arnold hoped to frighten the city into submission by a show of force, however, he was soon disappointed. The garrison had ample food and munitions to withstand a fairly lengthy siege, and a determined Scotsman named Colonel Allan MacLean had greatly strengthened the defenses and rallied the morale of the people of Quebec.

The residents of Quebec climbed the walls of the fortress to stare at the ragged band of soldiers that had come so far to conquer their city. The Canadians greeted the American troops in a peculiar way—they gave a loud and lusty cheer. The Americans returned the huzza. A few of Arnold's men fired at the garrison, but they were far out of range, and their shots fell short of the mark. The Canadians began to shell the Americans with cannon balls, but their barrage was as harmless as that of their foes. As each ball landed ineffectively on the plain, the Americans gave a loud cheer. That pattern continued for some time before Arnold, fearing that an errant shot might accidentally hit one of his men, withdrew his forces. The first meeting between the ad-

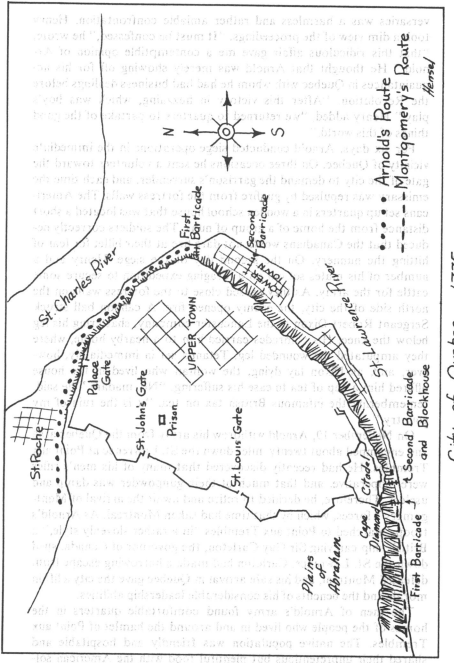

City of Quebec – 1775

•••••• Arnold's Route
– – – Montgomery's Route

Hersel

St. Charles River

St. Lawrence River

First Barricade

Second Barricade

LOWER TOWN

UPPER TOWN

Palace Gate

St. Roche

St. John's Gate

Prison

St. Louis' Gate

Citadel

Cape Diamond

Plains of Abraham

Second Barricade and Blockhouse

First Barricade

N · S

versaries was a harmless and rather amiable confrontation. Henry took a dim view of the proceedings. "It must be confessed," he wrote, "that this ridiculous affair gave me a contemptible opinion of Arnold." He thought that Arnold was merely showing off for his acquaintances in Quebec with whom he had had business dealings before the Revolution. "After this victory in huzzaing, which was boy's play," Henry added, "we returned to quarters to partake of the good things of this world."

For six days, Arnold conducted siege operations in the immediate vicinity of Quebec. On three occasions he sent a volunteer toward the gate of the city to demand the garrison's surrender, and each time the emissary was repulsed by gunfire from the fortress walls. The Americans set up quarters in a wooden school house that was located a short distance from the home of a group of nuns. The soldiers correctly deduced that the Canadians would not dare fire at their billet for fear of hitting the nunnery. On the second day of the siege, Henry and a number of his mates set out on a foraging expedition to secure some cattle for the army. As they passed close to the fortress walls on the north side of the city, the enemy opened fire. A cannon ball struck Sergeant Robert Dixon of the Lancaster company, shattering his leg below the knee. His comrades carried him to a nearby home, where they amputated the wounded leg. Tetanus set in immediately, however, and, as Dixon lay dying, the woman who lived in the house offered him a cup of tea to ease his suffering. "No, madam," he said, remembering the infamous British tax on tea, "it is the ruin of my country."

On November 19, Arnold withdrew his army from the Quebec area and encamped about twenty miles down the St. Lawrence at Point aux Trembles. He had recently discovered that many of his men's rifles were inoperative, and that much of their gunpowder was damp and useless. Therefore, he decided to retire and await the arrival of Montgomery's forces, which by that time had taken Montreal. As Arnold's troops marched to Point aux Trembles "in a rather slovenly style," a British ship carrying Sir Guy Carleton, the governor of Canada, sped down the St. Lawrence. Carleton had made a harrowing escape from defeated Montreal, and his safe arrival in Quebec gave the city a lift in morale and the benefits of his considerable leadership abilities.

The men of Arnold's army found comfortable quarters in the homes of the people who lived in and around the hamlet of Point aux Trembles. The native population was friendly and hospitable and shared their unpretentious but plentiful food with the American soldiers. The most distressing inconvenience of the men was the penetrating cold of the Canadian winter. Many wore only ragged and torn summer clothing that was hardly adequate in the bitter wind and driving snow.

In Search of Food and Clothing

In search of warm clothing, Henry and a few of his companions undertook a plundering expedition. They received information from a local resident that the nearby country home of Quebec's Lieutenant Governor Hector Theophilus Cramahe was stocked with an abundance of needed supplies. Under the leadership of Lieutenant Steele, a band of Lancastrians made their way in small carriages to Cramahe's summer residence.

They knocked on the door of the mansion, and the lieutenant governor's housekeeper, an Irishwoman, whom Henry described as "the largest and most brawny" woman he had ever seen, answered. The woman offered no resistance and led the Americans into a well-supplied kitchen, where five or six Canadian servants "huddled in the corner . . . trembling with fear." The men found the kitchen brimming "with those articles which good livers think necessary to the happy enjoyment of life," and also sighted a trap door that led to further treasures. They descended into the cellar and discovered stores of savory foodstuffs, including butter, lard, tallow and fine cuts of beef and pork. While the others foraged in the cellar, Henry remained in the kitchen, keeping a watchful eye on the servants with his rifle cocked. Hoping to trap the Americans in the cellar, the Irish housekeeper frequently invited Henry to join his companions; but he recognized her ploy and refused to heed her suasion.

After the party had "thoroughly gutted" the kitchen and cellar and loaded the supplies in the carriages, they returned to the house to search the other rooms. From the bedrooms they carried beds, spreads and blankets, leaving "not a jot behind." From the dining room, they took several sets of expensive cutlery, including a collection of dessert knives. The men noticed a finely finished mahogany couch in one room; and, although they lacked space for the entire piece, they seized the cushions, which were "equally elegant as the couch." Finally, after they had filled the carriages and hauled away anything that might be remotely useful, they departed. As they left, the housekeeper profusely thanked them for their "moderation," but Henry doubted the sincerity of her expressions of gratitude.

A few days later, Henry participated in another foray that procured cattle, pigs and poultry for the American forces. The young Lancastrian felt rather guilty about the plundering, describing the second expedition as a "disreputable exploit." His conscience was eased, however, by the fact that he and his mates had pillaged only "those who were notoriously tories."

Arrival of General Montgomery

On December 2, 1775, General Richard Montgomery arrived at Point aux Trembles from Montreal. He brought with him about three hundred soldiers, a few cannon and, best of all, the promise of warm clothing. Arnold's forces were impressed by the appearance and demeanor of Richard Montgomery. The general's arrival, Henry wrote, "gave us warmth and animation. He was well limbed, tall and handsome, though his face was much pockmarked. His air and manner designated the real soldier."

Montgomery and Arnold immediately began to make plans for the assault on Quebec. The general quickly perceived that the city could not be reduced by a siege. The American army was too small, and its artillery was too weak and ineffective to conduct a successful siege. Although Montgomery was keenly aware of the dangers and high casualty rates that would result from storming the garrison, he realized it was the only way to conquer Quebec. On December 23, the American officers met with Montgomery and agreed to attack the fortress at the earliest opportunity. They planned to strike on the first night that it was dark enough and snowing hard enough to shroud the movements of the troops. The next three days were distressingly clear, but on December 27, a brisk snowstorm began to fall. Montgomery issued orders to attack that night, and the American forces prepared for the assault.

But the plans fizzled. Just before the first troops were scheduled to move out, the snow stopped and the sky cleared. The Americans also discovered that two British informers had slipped out of camp to warn the garrison of the impending offensive. One was an American deserter, and the other was a Canadian prisoner who had escaped while the soldiers were preoccupied with preparing for the attack. Once the absence of the defectors was noticed, Montgomery knew that he had lost the element of surprise that was so essential to his strategy. Prudently, he decided that he had no alternative but to postpone the assault.

Time was now a matter of critical importance to Montgomery. Food supplies were starting to run low, and some men had contracted smallpox, arousing fears that the army would be decimated by the dread disease. But the general's greatest source of concern was that the term of enlistment for many of his troops would expire on December 31. An alarming number of men gave every indication that they intended to return to Massachusetts as soon as their enlistment had terminated. As Henry noted, "The patriotism of the summer of seventy-five, seemed almost extinguished in the winter of seventy-six." The Pennsylvania riflemen agreed to stay with Montgomery even if the others retreated. But the general knew that the departure of a significant portion of his army would deal a fatal blow to his campaign, and he anxiously watched the skies for signs of snow. To his relief, a heavy snowstorm, accompanied by howling winds and gloomy darkness, began on the evening of December 30. Montgomery issued orders to attack, and at two o'clock on the morning of December 31 the army moved out.

The Attack

There were two possible methods of assaulting Quebec. One was to storm the garrison's walls, which would require the American troops to scale the fortress with ladders, drive back the defenders, and force their way into the heart of the city, called the Upper Town. Montgomery knew that such a mode of attack stood little chance of success. The city's artillery would inflict heavy casualties on the American forces as they approached the fortress, and the walls were well protected by formidable numbers of enemy soldiers.

Montgomery sent a small detachment of troops to divert the garrison's attention by feinting a frontal assault, but he directed his major thrust at the section of the city called the Lower Town. The Lower Town bordered on the St. Lawrence River and consisted of docks, warehouses, crowded houses, narrow streets and blind alleys. It was less heavily defended than the central part of the city, but the barricades and gates that guarded its limited access to the Upper Town made it much easier to protect. A few sharpshooters with muskets and cannon could rain a deadly barrage on anyone who tried to scale the barricades or advance through the narrow streets. Montgomery was cognizant of the grim dangers of attacking the Lower Town, but he was convinced that it was less hazardous and more likely to succeed than a direct assault.

The assault at the second barricade.

Montgomery and Arnold agreed on a plan for assailing the fortress. The general would lead his veterans from the Montreal campaign around the high cliffs on the south side of the city and fight his way across two barricades into the Lower Town. Arnold would take the forces he had led up the Kennebec around the north side of Quebec, pass through the docks and warehouses along the river, and overcome two barricades that stood along his route. The two forces would reunite at Mountain Street in the Lower Town and jointly storm the gates that opened the way to the Upper Town.

The American strategy was well conceived and carefully planned, but the attack on Quebec was disastrous. Montgomery's contingent made their way with difficulty along the narrow path below the cliffs on the south side of Quebec. They reached the first barricade without being detected, and a few men hastily sawed through the wooden palisade. They moved on to the second barricade and cut through it as quickly and quietly as possible. Now only a guardhouse stood between the American troops and the Lower Town.

The defenders inside the guardhouse warily watched the shadowy movements of the advancing enemy. They waited as long as possible and then raked the narrow passage with a deadly volley of musket and cannon fire. Five men at the head of the American column fell, including General Montgomery, who was mortally wounded by a shot through the head. The barrage left the Americans disarrayed and leaderless. The command devolved upon Colonel Donald Campbell, who had seen enough of war and death. He ordered his men to retreat, and they hurriedly retraced their route. There would be no rendezvous with Arnold in the Lower Town.

Meanwhile, Arnold and his men were encountering difficulties. As they moved along the north side of the city, marksmen within the fortress opened fire with muskets and cannon, inflicting numerous casualties on the American column. The driving snow impaired the vision of the American forces and made footing extremely precarious. As they stumbled through the dockyards, Private Henry fell headlong into a gaping cavity that he thought was either a drydock or a sawpit. "My descent was terrible; gun and all was involved in a great depth of snow," he wrote. Henry suffered a "violent contusion" on the knee and got separated from his friends. He scrambled out of the pit into which he had fallen, but the soldiers who filed by had little sympathy for his plight. They refused to give him a place in line, and he finally had to take a place near the rear of the column.

Meanwhile, the men at the head of the column had reached the first barricade. The enemy opened fire. The casualties they inflicted included Benedict Arnold, who caught a musket ball on his left leg. The wound was not severe, but it bled profusely and so weakened the colonel that he could not stand or walk without assistance. Arnold shouted encouragement to his troops as they filed by, but the loss of his leadership was a blow to the morale of the army. As a pair of soldiers helped Arnold to the rear, Daniel Morgan assumed command. Within a short time, the Americans surmounted the first barricade and captured its defenders.

Now only one barricade stood between Arnold's forces and the anticipated rendezvous with Montgomery. For a fleeting moment, the gate of the palisade stood open and undefended, but a British detachment quickly moved down from the Upper Town and took up positions behind the twelve-foot barricade. The Americans struggled valiantly to overcome the enemy resistance, but they were constantly repelled by the deadly fusillade that the British fired into the narrow passage. Eventually, they had to seek refuge in the houses along the street.

Meanwhile, Governor Carleton had sent a detachment of troops out the main gate of the city. They traced the route of Arnold's forces around the north side of Quebec and marched to the site of the first barricade, blocking the only available path of retreat for the American forces. Trapped in the cramped area between the two barricades and unable to advance in either direction, the Americans had no alternative but to surrender. The assault on Quebec, the city they had come so far to conquer, had failed.

The Bitter Fruit of Defeat

About sixty Americans died in the attack, and over four hundred were taken prisoner, including John Joseph Henry. Those soldiers who escaped death and captivity regrouped as best they could under the command of Benedict Arnold and awaited the arrival of reinforcements to lay siege to Quebec.

Governor Carleton was a gracious victor. The American wounded received prompt and compassionate medical attention, and the dead were treated respectfully. General Montgomery's body was recovered and given a dignified burial commensurate with his rank. The British separated the American prisoners by rank and sent the officers to be incarcerated in a seminary within the city walls. Private Henry was grouped with the enlisted men, who were questioned about their

St. John's Gate

names and places of birth by a British colonel named McDougal. Strangely enough, Henry knew McDougal, whom he had met on a visit to his uncle in Detroit three years before. The colonel was a close friend of his uncle and was "naturally polite and kindhearted." When he interrogated Henry, the young American reminded him of their previous acquaintance and, hoping to receive better treatment from his captors, asked to be interned with the officers. McDougal was surprised and rather pleased to see Henry, but he denied the request. "No, my dear boy," he said, "you had better remain where you are; the officers, as you are in rebellion, may be sent to England, and there be tried for treason."

Henry and the other enlisted men were confined in the basement of a huge monastery inside the gates of Quebec. A short time after they arrived there, Governor Carleton sent them a "New Year's gift" of a large quantity of beer, bread and cheese. "It was a present which exhilarated our hearts and drew from us much thankfulness," Henry recalled.

The British continued to accord their American prisoners humane treatment as the days and weeks passed. The food they gave the captives was neither appetizing nor plentiful, but the entire city was short on provisions, and the British were remarkably generous in sharing what they had with the Americans. Henry and his comrades received as their daily allotment a coarse biscuit "the size of a cake of gingerbread," a half to three-quarters of a pound of heavily salted pork or beef, butter that became increasingly rancid, molasses and vinegar. "From all information attainable on our part," Henry wrote, "we were as well treated as those of the garrison, who lived on the same kinds of food, except as to liquor, which deprivation was more beneficial than injurious to our men."

Henry's provisions were augmented by the additional biscuits given him by Henry Crone of York County. To relieve the tedium of prison existence, many of the men took up gambling. Since they had no money or valuables, they wagered with biscuits. Crone was an experienced, devoted and skillful gambler and often stayed up all night "contending for a biscuit with as much spirit and heat as probably he had done in former times for fifty or a hundred dollars." Crone was a consistent winner and, because he liked Henry, often gave him ten, fifteen or even as many as thirty biscuits that he had won. At times, when Crone's luck or skill deserted him, he had to reclaim some of the biscuits from Henry, but that was an infrequent occurrence.

A few days after the Americans were imprisoned, the British

conveyed a message to Henry from Captain Daniel Morgan, who was, of course, incarcerated with the officers. Morgan liked Henry and invited him to come stay in the seminary where the officers were confined. Morgan already had secured Governor Carleton's consent to transfer Henry, but the young Lancastrian demurred. He remembered the warning of the kindly Colonel McDougal and was wary of joining the officers. Furthermore, his only clothes were the ones he wore on his back, and they were so tattered that he thought his "savage covering" would be inappropriate among men of rank. Henry also declined Morgan's invitation because most of his close friends were not with the officers in the seminary. Finally, the Americans were already thinking of trying to escape from prison, and Henry believed that the enlisted men were "in a much superior situation for such a purpose, than that of the seminary."

Plans For Escape

In mid-March, 1776, the British moved the American enlisted men from the basement of the monastery where they had been confined to the Dauphin jail. The transfer to the Dauphin jail strengthened the resolve of the American soldiers to attempt an escape, because the prison stood a mere three hundred yards from the walls of the city. The prisoners also soon discovered that the bars on the windows were poorly fitted and corroded and could easily be removed. They found several large iron hoops carelessly left about by their captors, and from them fashioned crude swords and spears. The men formed a committee, of which Henry was a member, to work out a plan of escape.

The scheme that the council agreed upon was exceedingly ambitious. It called for a coordinated effort between the escaping prisoners inside the city walls and Arnold's forces who were still encamped outside Quebec. At the appointed hour, the prisoners would burst out of the windows and doors of the jail, overcome the sentries, and set fire to the prison and the buildings surrounding it. The fires would be a signal to Arnold to begin an attack on the city from without. The object was to occupy the attention of the enemy while the American captives dashed to safety through the gates of the fortress. The success of the plot depended upon maintaining strict secrecy, finding a way to inform Arnold of the plan, and procuring a supply of powder to set the fires.

The prisoners got word to Arnold of the impending uprising when one of their number, John Martin, made a daring escape. The men had concealed an outfit of white clothing in a secluded place in the prison yard, and one evening, as they were going from the yard back to the cell block, created a commotion that allowed Martin to steal away unnoticed and hide in an obscure corner of the prison yard. He slipped on the white garments and, after waiting until the wind and cold of the night drove the sentries into the shelter of their guard houses, scaled both the prison walls and the city walls. One British soldier fired at him as he climbed the walls of the city, but he jumped to safety into the deep snow below, where his white clothes obliterated him from view. The prison officials, who were not meticulous administrators, failed to notice Martin's absence.

Meanwhile, the American conspirators were gathering and storing gunpowder. They built tiny toy cannons of folded paper and thread and purchased from prison guards small quantities of powder to fire the play howitzers, which gave off a "blaze and report . . . nearly as great and as loud as that of small pistols." The British seemed pleased that the Americans had contrived such a harmless way to amuse themselves, failing to realize that the prisoners were using the toy cannons as a pretext to procure powder for more serious purposes. The Americans obtained more powder than they needed for their games and sequestered the excess supplies for use in their escape attempt. They paid for the powder with money they received from kind-hearted citizens of Quebec. Some local residents, especially "pious matrons" and nuns, took pity on the captives, visited them in prison, and gave them small sums of money to buy a few luxuries.

On one occasion, Henry and a friend named Thomas Gibson took advantage of a generous and unsuspecting nun to secure funds for powder. Gibson had the good fortune to remain in much better health than his comrades; and, in contrast to their pale and wan appearance, "his cheeks were blooming as roses." One day, after Henry and Gibson saw a nun approaching the prison, Gibson leaped into bed fully clothed and covered himself with blankets so that only his head was visible. Henry met the nun at the door of the prison and beseeched her to visit the bedside of his friend. When the nun saw Gibson, she was greatly disturbed, because she thought his red cheeks indicated that he had an alarmingly high fever. She crossed herself and whispered a prayer and then pressed into Gibson's hand all the money she had in her purse. "It was well the lady was no physician," Henry commented. The ruse was a source of hilarity and "extreme merriment," and all the money was used to buy more powder.

Thick ice blocks the doorway to escape.

35

The Plot Discovered

In the end, all the preparations for the escape were in vain. On the night before the Americans had planned to stage their sortie, two New England soldiers who were not privy to the plot made a blundering attempt to escape on their own. The British easily caught them and immediately doubled the prison's guard.

The next morning the prison administrators visited the other American captives, who assured them that there was no general plan to escape and that they had known nothing of the effort of the unfortunate New Englanders. The officers accepted that explanation and were preparing to depart when a "vile informer" stepped forward and asked to see them in private. "Sir," he said, "I have something to disclose." The informer told the British of the entire plot and named the conspiracy's leaders. A short time later, the guards appeared with irons, shackles and handcuffs and manacled the American prisoners. A few Americans, including Henry, remained unfettered only because the British ran short of handcuffs and shackles. Most of the captives soon found ways surreptitiously to free themselves from the irons, but the British were now much more alert and suspicious, and the chances for escape were irrevocably lost.

In the middle of April, after three and a half months of captivity, an acute form of scurvy spread among the American prisoners, accompanied by severe diarrhea, large and ugly black blotches caused by bleeding under the skin, loosening of gums, and, in many cases, loss of teeth. "The hilarity and fun which supported our spirits in the greatest misfortunes," Henry wrote, "gave way to wailing, groaning and death." The British did the best they could to alleviate the distress of the Americans. They sent a doctor to attend the ailing prisoners and, to the extent possible for the besieged city, provided them with fresh vegetables to combat the illness. Governor Carleton, whom Henry thought "did every thing . . . which an honest man and a good Christian could," ordered that the men be supplied with fresh beef and gave each of the prisoners a new linen shirt.

In early May, several ships reached Quebec with provisions and reinforcements for the garrison. The siege of the city ended, and the American forces hastily retreated. But the arrival of the supplies had happy consequences for the prisoners, who received fresh bread, good meat and abundant quantities of vegetables. A short time later, the British removed the irons and shackles from the captives, and the Americans spent hours playing strenuous games, both to amuse themselves and to counteract the effects of scurvy. Many of the men, especially those who constantly exercised, felt better, but the scurvy still lingered on. When Henry lay down at night after playing ball all day, he suffered excruciating pain that lasted for two hours. Although exercise and an improved diet relieved the symptoms of the scurvy, Henry believed that it could only be cured when he and the others received their freedom, "that greatest of blessings."

Home to Lancaster

At long last, in August of 1776, the American captives learned that an exchange of prisoners had been negotiated and that they were going to be released. On August 10, after more than seven months in detention, the survivors of the Quebec expedition sailed down the St. Lawrence, bound for New York and home. Unlike the arduous journey up the Kennebec to Quebec, the voyage home was easy and uneventful; and the ships arrived in New York harbor on September 11.

To the dismay of the American soldiers, however, they discovered that they could not disembark. The British army had recently triumphed over American forces in the Battle of Long Island, and the status of the Quebec veterans remained uncertain. Some feared that they would again become British prisoners.

On the evening of September 22, after eleven days of detention in New York harbor, the Americans were shocked to see flames shooting skyward from the city. A huge fire, fanned by a brisk breeze, was ravaging New York. Although the ship was anchored four miles from the city, "the deck . . . for many hours was lighted as at noon day." Henry initially suspected the British of starting the blaze, but quickly concluded that Americans were responsible because the British worked diligently to control the fire and assist those trapped in it. The burning of New York, he believed, was eloquent testimony to the tragedy and injustice of war. "Baseness and villainy are the growth of all climes, and of all nations," Henry commented.

Finally, after weeks of anxious waiting, the Americans received permission to leave the ships and make their way to safety and freedom. With unmitigated joy and gratitude, the men rowed a short distance in small boats to Elizabethtown [now Elizabeth], New Jersey. "Singing, dancing, the Indian halloo, in short, every species of vociferousness was adopted by the men . . . to express their extreme pleasure." Henry, like all his comrades, was penniless, and he was worried about

The city of New York ablaze.

how he was going to get home to Lancaster. Fortunately, he sighted "a wagon built in Lancaster county fashion" that carried supplies to the American army. The owner of the wagon greeted him warmly and told him that his friends and family had assumed he was dead. He lent Henry two dollars, and the young man immediately set out for home. Within four days he reached Lancaster, where he was joyously re-united with his parents.

Henry's appetite for adventure and his desire to fight for inde-pendence still were not satisfied, and he happily accepted a com-mission as a captain in the Virginia militia that Daniel Morgan secured for him. His opportunity for further military service was abruptly terminated, however, when a virulent recurrence of the scurvy struck him a short time after his return home. The disease centered in the knee he had injured in the assault on Quebec. Henry's leg became inflamed and infected, and he also was afflicted by a de-bilitating bone disease. For two years, he lay bedridden and unable to walk; and, even after he recovered, he could walk only with the sup-port of a cane. During his confinement, he read constantly and also talked with a number of revolutionary leaders who occasionally stayed in his father's home, including Benjamin Franklin, Thomas Paine and David Rittenhouse.

After his lengthy recuperation, Henry served for a time as a law clerk's apprentice in Lancaster. Then he took up the study of law and was admitted to the bar in 1785. Eight years later, Governor Thomas Mifflin of Pennsylvania appointed him judge of the state's second judi-cial district, which included Lancaster, York, Chester and Dauphin Counties.

Henry's health remained precarious, and in 1804 he began to suffer increasingly frequent and severe attacks of gout. Finally, in the latter part of 1810, his ailments forced him to resign his judgeship and retire from public life.

At about the same time, he began to dictate his recollections of the expedition to Quebec to his daughter. The judge was moved to record his account of the campaign in part because his suffering recalled to mind the hardships and privations of his earlier experiences. He may also have been concerned by the growing tensions between the United States and England, which eventually culminated in the War of 1812. Henry's tale is replete with admonishments about the horror and tragedy of war.

The judge's health rapidly deteriorated, and he completed his story just a short time before he died in Lancaster on April 15, 1811, at the age of 53. Although the old man's memory at times failed him on events that occurred thirty-five years before, his account of the march to Quebec was a proud and lasting monument to a courageous and heroic group of American patriots.

Editor's Note

J. Samuel Walker, Ph.D., is an instructor in American History at the University College, University of Maryland. He is the author of a forthcoming book on American Foreign Policy and of articles on anti-war movements and foreign policy. He suggests the following for further reading on the Quebec Campaign: The basic source for this essay was John Joseph Henry's *Account of Arnold's Campaign Against Quebec*. Although originally published in Lancaster in 1812, it frequently has been reprinted. The novelist Kenneth Roberts has compiled and annotated fourteen journals from the Quebec campaign, including Henry's, in *March to Quebec: Journals of the Members of Arnold's Expedition* (Garden City, New York, 1938). The best general history of the expedition is Harrison Bird, *Attack on Quebec: The American Invasion of Canada, 1775* (New York, 1968). Allen French, *The First Year of the American Revolution* (Boston, 1934), also contains valuable information on Arnold's campaign.

Lancaster County
in the
American Revolution

The official Bicentennial Book series is ~~~~~~~~~~ Lancaster County Bicentennial Committee in an effort to preserve the rich heritage of the greater Lancaster area during the American Revolution. Seven books are planned for the series, each revealing a different aspect of the County's participation.

BOOKS IN SERIES

A WAY OF LIFE by Jim Kinter with illustrations by Michael Abel.

While the Lancaster area was not the site of any military engagements in the Revolution, its men saw action from Boston to Yorktowne. The area played the important role of supplying war materiel and served as a training ground for troops and campsite for prisoners and wounded.
1974   64pp.   5½ x 8½   L.C. 74–29188   ISBN 0–915010–04–6   paper $2.00

THE PENNSYLVANIA RIFLE by Samuel E. Dyke with illustrations by Constantine Kermes.

The history of the Pennsylvania–Kentucky Rifle is traced from the hunting rifle of the German settlers, to the Lancaster County gunsmiths, to their ultimate use in the American Revolution by the Continental Army.
1974   64pp.   5½ x 8½   L.C. 74–29189   ISBN 0–915010–05–4   paper $2.00

FIGHTING THE BATTLES: LANCASTER'S SOLDIERS MARCH OFF TO WAR by Frederic Shriver Klein with illustrations by Florence S. Taylor.

Lancaster's riflemen, armed with the famed "Pennsylvania Rifle" from local gunsmiths' shops, quickly established a reputation for marksmanship. Various battles in which Lancastrians participated (all outside the boundaries of Lancaster County) are discussed.
1975   56pp.   5½ x 8½   L.C. 75–15438   ISBN 0–915010–06–2   paper $2.00

— continued —

THE PERILS OF PATRIOTISM: JOHN JOSEPH HENRY AND THE AMERICAN ATTACK ON QUEBEC, 1775 by J. Samuel Walker with illustrations by Joann W. Hensel.

An account of the 1775–1776 American Army campaign against Quebec is given as it was seen by a young Lancaster County soldier of seventeen, fighting with Benedict Arnold's forces.
1975 56pp. 5½ × 8½ L.C. 75–15439 ISBN 0–915010–08–9 paper $2.00

FORTHCOMING TITLES

The Revolutionary Leadership by G. Terry Madonna with illustrations by Henry Libhart.

The Military Marketbasket by John W. W. Loose with illustrations by Michael Abel.

Prisoners, Pacifists and Loyalists by Rollin C. Steinmetz with illustrations by Grace Steinmetz.

All of the above books as well as the handsome, full-color Bicentennial Calendars may be ordered direct from the co-publisher, postpaid.

Mail to : SUTTER HOUSE
        BOX 146
        LITITZ, PA. 17543

ORDER FORM

Please send me the following Bicentennial Books:

———— copies A WAY OF LIFE by Jim Kinter @ $2.00
———— copies THE PENNSYLVANIA RIFLE by Samuel E. Dyke @ $2.00
———— copies FIGHTING THE BATTLES by Frederic S. Klein @ $2.00
———— copies THE PERILS OF PATRIOTISM by J. Samuel Walker @ $2.00

Please send me the following Bicentennial Calendars:

———— copies 1975 (limited quantity available) @ $2.50
———— copies 1976 folded calendar (12 × 18 open) @ $3.00
———— copies 1976 large, non-folding calendar (12 × 18 open). Edition limited to 5000 copies @ $3.50

I enclose $———— (Pa. residents please add 6% sales tax.)

☐ Please place me on your mailing list for future announcements.

        NAME ————————————————————————

        ADDRESS ——————————————————————

                ————————————————————————